Cruising and Sketching Baja

Cruising

NORTHLAND PRESS / FLAGSTAFF

and Sketching Baja

by Annette Scott

FIRST EDITION

ISBN 0-87358-123-7

Library of Congress Catalog Card Number 73-93994

Composed and Printed in the United States of America

To Don Scott

The Route of
the Yacht *Annette*

San Diego

Ensenada

Isla San Martín

MEXICO

Punta San Carlos

Punta Canoas

SEA OF CORTEZ

BAJA CALIFORNIA

Isla Cedros

Turtle Bay

Guaymas

Santa Rosalía

Punta Chivata

Punta Abreojos

Punta Púlpito

San Juanico

Loreto

Bahía Escondido

Agua Verde

Punta Pequeña

PACIFIC OCEAN

Isla San Francisco

Bahía Santa María

Isla Partida

Bahía Magdalena

Isla Espíritu Santo

Pichilinque

La Paz

Bahía Los Muertos

Bahía Los Frailes

Cabo San Lucas

N

Contents

Preface

THIS BOOK WAS WRITTEN for the pleasure of those who have traveled these waters and for those who would like to. The sketches were made with felt pen and watercolors, often from the deck as the boat was underway. They were shared with other boaters, and the text grew from comments about these sketches.

Don Scott learned to sail as a young boy on Georgian Bay in Canada. In 1920 he built a canoe with a sail and used it to explore the lakes of Arizona. Later, he built a motor sailer in the back yard of his home in Phoenix, sewing the sails in the spacious attic. This boat was launched in the Gulf of California. During the 1960's he had a forty-two-foot Drake power boat, the *Charl Don*, and enjoyed many vacation fishing trips in the Gulf. He always hoped to cruise the Pacific coast of Baja.

I was a newcomer to boating, and came aboard my husband's fifty-four-foot DeFever cruiser armed only with a sketch pad, rubber-soled shoes, and a cook book entitled *The Compleat Mess*. On our first trip Don taught me how to pilot and navigate. Between cruises we attended San Diego Power Squadron classes in Seamanship, and then headed into the Pacific for Mexican waters.

On the Pacific and since our return many people have suggested and supported the idea of this book. Among them are our friends on boats who encouraged me from the beginning by their interest, and who contributed comments and local knowledge. Among these are the people of the boats *Dulcita IV, Evening Star, Sou'wester, Patience, Princess, Apogee, Desiarto, Seacomber, Moana, Gitano* and *Dreamboat.*

Appreciation is also expressed to Al and Floy Fuller who shared our first adventure on the west coast of Baja, and to Paul Holz, Tom Mautner and Ann Martinet of San Diego.

My thanks to my mother, Mrs. Helen Empfield, for correcting my spelling; Nancy Phillips and Helen Bergen for proofreading, and Anita Ramas de Schaff, our Spanish teacher in Phoenix. To Ina May Moore, Clara Nichols, Marge Young and Lily Ham of Phoenix for opening to me the fun and freedom of watercolor.

From all this has come a book of fun and good memories. Join us *Cruising and Sketching Baja.*

ANNETTE SCOTT

x

*Fog moved into the harbor on the
morning we fueled for the trip. The
boats of the San Diego Yacht Club, seen
from the fuel dock, were framed by the
stern window.*

    *Sky and water were all one color,
and the only thing moving was a little
family of ducks.*

8a.m. From the Fuel Dock SDYC Feb. 27, 1972

A newcomer to boating becomes interested in the origins of nautical terms. As early as the year 1600 men were measuring the speed of a ship by throwing a chip, or small log of wood, overboard at the bow, watching to see how long it took to float to the stern.

Later a line was attached to the log with knots tied at intervals. As the knots slipped through the seaman's hands they were counted. We dragged a "taff-rail log" behind, which showed our speed to be about ten knots.

Distance came to be measured in "knots" at sea, and the length of a nautical mile was eventually agreed upon, and now is universally used by commercial airliners, oil tankers and weekend boaters.

A depth indicator in the pilot house

told us how deep the water was under the boat. When it went out of order, we improvised a lead line by tying knots every six feet along a fishing line. Securing a paperweight to the end of the line, we dropped it into the water, measuring depth in the anchorages from Ensenada to Cabo San Lucas. "This boat is an Offshore Cruiser," the Skipper said, "so let's keep it off shore!"

We traveled the route of migrating whales and saw their smoky fountains blowing. A huge double fluke soared above the surface and disappeared.

We dropped anchor in the harbor at Ensenada, México. Looking around we discovered one of the joys of boating — friends on other boats in the same harbor. We had pot-luck supper aboard and swapped stories.

Encenada Harbor March 2

A small tug boat brought this giant freighter into the harbor the day we went ashore to check with the Port Captain and Immigration Office.

Up anchor and away the next morning to find the weather outside the harbor very windy and the sea too rough for comfort. We turned back to Ensenada to wait for better weather. "Throw out the sacks of trash," the Skipper said, "this is known as a 'garbage' run!"

Tug Boat – Ensenada

–Annette Scott

Isla San Martín is a cone-shaped volcanic island with a dependable navigation light on top. Dozens of seals make their home in the lagoon and countless birds cluster on the whitened rocks.

Anchored in "Hassler's Cove" behind the natural breakwater, we saw pelicans, sea gulls and cormorants. They swept by in formation and disappeared beyond the island hills.

In the night the phosphorescent water made the fish luminous as they darted and flashed around the boat.

Lagoon at San Martin - Jan. 23 1973

On the run from Isla San Martín to
Bahía San Carlos the gauge on the
water-maker indicated that no water was
being distilled from the sea. After
several frustrating hours in the engine
room it started to function again.
''Happiness,'' said the Skipper, ''is a
water tank that runneth over!''

We entered Bahía San Carlos with a
tired little bird riding on the forward
deck. The surf ran unbroken for miles
along the lonely shore, its white crest
looking like the manes of white horses
charging from the sea.

Rain seldom falls on beautiful Isla Cedros but clouds on its volcanic mountain peaks give enough moisture to nourish a forest of cedar trees.

Fresh water from the springs of this island made it a watering place for early explorers, whalers, and pirates.

A colony of sea lions inhabits the eastern shore about two miles below the north Cedros lighthouse. Their barking is continuous day and night. With the dinghy anchored close off shore we recorded the sound of their mournful voices. We heard a duet in two keys against the background chorus. When the tape was played back they answered it.

Bahía Tortuga (Turtle Bay) is part of Bahía San Bartolomé. Near the southern entrance there are several huge rocks. One is called "Coffin Rock" because of its shape, and it has a light on it.

Seeing that this light was not burning one night when he sailed in, Lynn Bayless, of the Apogee, rowed over in his dinghy the next day. He discovered an osprey's nest completely filling the beacon.

He climbed up the monstrous rock, fought off the birds and removed the nest. Our Skipper now likes to call it "Lynn's Light."

P.S. The birds waited at a distance, with sticks in their beaks. By the time Lynn got back to his boat they were rebuilding the nest.

- Annette Scott

Lynn's Light - Turtle Bay
March 21, 1972

You may recall the Triton, one of two rafts which set out to go around the world by drifting with the currents. The Triton became a fueling barge in Turtle Bay and belonged to Gordo whose autograph is on this sketch.

When fueling from Gordo's Barge, we felt a certain urgency. The Skipper said,

"Let's get over there and get our fuel before she sinks!"

Late in 1972 the Triton did sink during a fierce Pacific storm. She went down to the bottom of the bay, barrels of diesel, black rubber tires, little oil lantern and all. Gordo now sells fuel off the dock.

@DANGERARDO TALAMANTZ

Gordo's Barge · Turtle Bay
· Annette Scott · Mar. '19

*María is one of Gordo's eleven friendly
children. She greeted us in English,
"Hello, how are you?" as we struggled
up the ladder to the dock in Turtle Bay.
She led us to the Post Office, the grocery,
and the bakery where they make
delicious raised doughnuts and
Mexican bread.*

*The clustered houses in the town
seemed newly painted in bright yellows,
green, purple, blue, pink and orange.
People on the streets were walking
toward the church where a tamale
dinner was in progress.*

Turtle Bay   June 1 '72
..Annette Scott

Pacific Standard Time changes to Mountain Standard at Turtle Bay because the coast of Baja runs southeast from San Diego. The principal fish cannery for the town, however, is located in Ensenada to the northwest, so Turtle Bay keeps Pacific Time. We set our watches back when leaving for Punta Abreojos.

Tuning in to Marine Radio 2638 we listened to the daily chatter of boaters traveling along the coasts of Baja.

...A woman had been rescued by helicopter at 25 north, 130 west.

...The Fridolph *requested that we try to contact the Padre at Ascunción Bay to watch for the tuna clipper,* San Juan.

...Dix Brow was headed north on Vixon *and would return in May to bring up the* Sou'wester.

...Bruce Barnes on his Qualifier *was now at "Mag Bay" and reported thirty knots wind.*

...Shorty Trim on the Peggy Lou *in Guaymas reported that Min Flicka would be in Turtle Bay in an hour.*

Along our route we talked by radio to a research vessel, the Thomas L. Thompson, *whose crew was investigating "upwellings" of water from the lower ocean depths.*

A porpoise water ballet was on the program for the day! Hundreds of porpoises played in our wake and around our bow, five and six at a time arching out of the water in unison. A turtle swam by, and a group of sea lions swung out of the water in porpoise formation.

The anchorage at Punta Pequeña in Bahía San Juanico is well remembered because it was so hard to find! It is remembered also because a full moon rose there as the sun went down, one in the east and one in the west, both red, and both the same size. For one bad moment we wondered, "Which way is east?"

One night at Punta Pequeña ours was the only boat at anchor, so it was startling to hear footsteps on the deck at two a.m. The Skipper rushed out by moonlight to find a huge bird on the bow rail!

Shrimp Boat at Pequeña

Thirty shrimp boats were anchored at Bahía San Juanico the next day, indicating that the weather was rough outside. The Skipper said, "If the shrimp boats stay in, we stay in."

Five of the crew of a shrimp boat stopped by in their dory on their way to the village for Fiesta. Later they returned singing, wet from a spill out of their dory, but happy and wishing to share their beer with us. We warmed them with café caliente and they gave us fresh

shrimp in return for our hospitality.
   Our toast of the evening was, Salud
Amor y Pesetas, y tiempo para
disfrutarlos. *(Health, Love, and Money,
and the time to enjoy them!)*

The first compass is said to have been a lodestone splinter thrust through a straw and floating in a container. When it was discovered that earth's magnetic north differed from true north as shown by the Pole Star, the Table of Variation was devised.

Forgetting the Variation when charting a course from Bahía San Juanico, I discovered my error when we were twenty miles off course. Changing course we finally saw Punta San Lázaro ahead and christened it the "twenty mile mountain." It looked beautiful to us as we dropped the hook with relief in Bahía Santa María at 1815, just before sunset.

The 20 Mile Mountain
Friday March 23

Called langostina *(little lobster) in México, these tiny creatures by the thousands are often found in María and Magdalena Bays. This one was dipped out of the water in a saucepan to sit for his portrait, and then returned to the* water. One claw is on a Mexican coin.

Scripps Institute of Oceanography at La Jolla identified him from our description as a kind of crab, genus: Pleuroncodes, species: Planipes. They are the food of the tuna fish. Tiny when

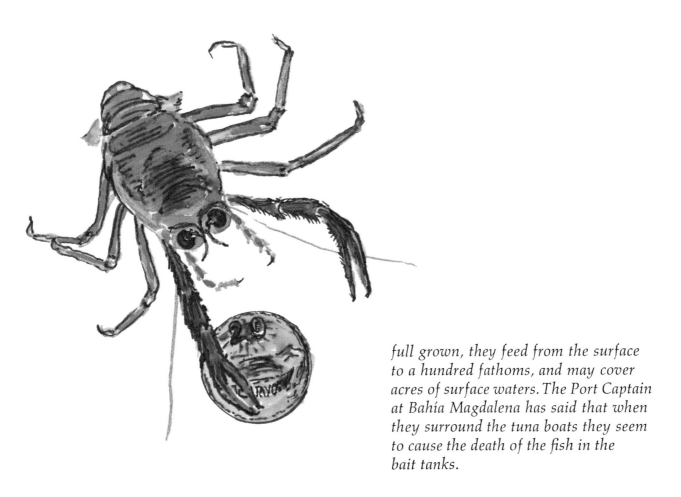

full grown, they feed from the surface to a hundred fathoms, and may cover acres of surface waters. The Port Captain at Bahía Magdalena has said that when they surround the tuna boats they seem to cause the death of the fish in the bait tanks.

Shrimp boats at anchor have their nets strung high above the decks to mend and dry.

Shrimp Boats at Mag Bay

— Annette Scott 3/2/73

Sea Mist *was a sail boat traveling north to Bahía Magdalena. Her engine died, and she was tossing in a heavy sea trying to beat her way against an unfavorable wind. We went down to stand by and tow if necessary.*

A school of porpoise encouraged us as we tried to sight the boat. When we saw her she was moving like a bucking bronco! Both skippers were relieved when she was able to make her way to "Mag Bay" unaided. Towing in a rough sea can be dangerous.

A boat is a complicated collection of systems and equipment. It carries its own fuel, water, provisions, and spare parts. There is no road map to pinpoint where you are, and no plumber to call if the drains are plugged!

All those who travel by water are well acquainted with "Murphy's Law of Boating."

MURPHY'S LAW

A. *On a boat there is never a time when everything works.*

B. *There is nothing on a boat that works all the time (except the Skipper and the "crew"!)*

Pelicans fly close to the water in majestic formation, skimming near the surface. One rises, turns, dives suddenly with neck outstretched and wings folding. He does a somersault under water and comes up with a fish. There is a hood-shaped protective covering on his head which often looks like a little fur cap.

Pelicans can move fast enough to catch

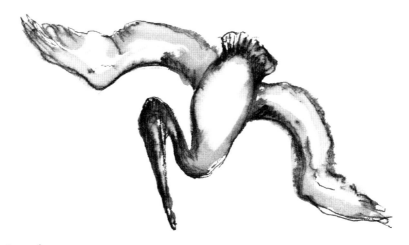

the bait on a fishing line being thrown
out. The fisherman finds himself reeling
in a pelican from the air! (This may
seem like one for the birds, but it is not
a fish story!)

It was an overnight run from Bahía Magdalena to Cabo San Lucas. We saw the mammoth Hotel Finisterra near the southern tip of the peninsula. It looked miniature among the rugged mountain formations.

I climbed to the Hotel Finisterra to enjoy the view of the Pacific. The radio had carried news of the racing sail boats competing in the International Yacht Race from San Diego to Acapulco. Their sails could not be seen passing the Cape that day because they were far off shore, hunting the winds that would carry them swiftly to Acapulco.

Pacific from the Hotel Finisterra
Cabo San Lucas

Annette Scott

There are towering rocks at the southern tip of Baja, called "Land's End." It is a place of golden sand, green water, white breakers, and twisted rock formations. Wind and surf here have carved a window to the Pacific.

Pacific Side of Land's End March 30

A fish cannery has been in continuous daily operation since 1929 at Cabo San Lucas. Fishermen throw their lines off the end of the fueling dock. Many a pleasure craft coming in to fuel has been asked to wait un momentito *till that yellowtail is pulled in.*

We saw a Mexican commercial fishing boat unloading its catch into the cannery.

Fuel Dock. Cabo San Lucas

CIA. DE PRODUCTOS MARINOS. &
PLANTA EMPACADORA
CABO SAN LUCAS, B. CALIF.

Annette Scott May 17

Maggie's Clothesline
- A. Scott

Back in 1961 when Al Fuller sailed into Cabo San Lucas, there was only the cannery, a cluster of shacks, a roofless structure atop the hill and a busy little woman named Maggie whose clothesline was always full.

Maggie takes in laundry from visiting boats, and the clothesline is now busier than ever since Maggie saved enough money to buy two washing machines.

Wash Day - Cabo San Lucas

Annette Scott
2-14-93

The bay is alive with boats; sport fishers, power boats, sail boats, cruise ships, and colorful Mexican tuna and shrimp boats.

A favorite amusement for the crews of anchored pleasure craft is observing the problems of other boaters getting the anchor down. A skipper and his mate seldom agree on just where to drop the anchor!

San Lucas Bay from Hotel Finisterra

Annette Scott 2-14-73

An independent tabby cat named Mimi lives aboard the Dreamboat *with Frank and Sue Eckert. She was brought aboard as a kitten and since then has never been off the boat.*

"When I first heard of Mimi on the radio," the Skipper said, "she was getting so much attention I thought she was Frank's wife!"

Dreamboat at Cabo San Lucas
February · 1978

We met Duggan at the Cape. He is a well-trained boat dog who never dirties the deck or the carpeting below. He is rowed ashore twice a day in a dinghy by his owners, Kermit and Fritz Parker of the Patience.

One night a bag of tools was left on the forward deck. The same night Duggan found a bowl of candy bars in the galley, which he ate, wrappers and all. He became very sick, but being a well-trained boat dog he would not soil the deck or the carpeting. He solved his problem by using the open tool bag on the forward deck!

Duggan Goes Ashore

Rubber Dory

Cabo San Lucas
X-16-73

The little town of Cabo San Lucas,
swept away by a hurricane in 1939, has
been rebuilt about a mile inland. By foot
or by cab, the boaters go to town to clear
their travel papers with the Port Captain
and the Immigration Office, to buy
supplies and gifts, obtain fueling
permits, and absorb a little of the
leisurely pace of Mexican life.

There is a small church across the street from the Kindergarten in Cabo San Lucas.

Annette Scott
2·14·73

Church of San Lucas

Leaving Cabo San Lucas we passed again the rocks of Land's End and headed north toward Bahía de Los Frailes. Here the Pacific waters meet the waters of the Gulf of California which is also known as the Sea of Cortez.

It seems fitting to recognize in this way the work of Hernando Cortez. He dispatched many voyages of discovery into the Gulf, the first one in 1528. The peninsula was then thought to be an island.

Cortez poured his personal resources into these voyages. To explore Baja California, he spent from his own pocket the equivalent of three million dollars today. He was not repaid by Spain and died broken in spirit. For centuries afterward other men acquired wealth and fame by following the routes which he established.

Maree Sea at Frailes Anchorage   Feb 22, '75

Annette Scott

Bahía Los Muertos means "Bay of the Dead." There are many stories about the origin of this name. One tale relates that a Chinese ship long ago sought refuge and medicine at the harbor of La Paz but was turned away because of Yellow Fever aboard. The ship left La Paz harbor and put in at this bay. All but a very few of the crew died and were buried here.

Los Muertos

Cruising along the way we passed many picturesque mountains and sport fishing resorts.

Approching Gorda Pt.
Los Picachitos

Hotel Las Cruces Palmilla from Northward

Annette Scott May 15

Arena Point

Punta Arena was not as near as it seems in this sketch! Our binoculars brought the structure closer as we cruised past.

These crosses are said to be replacements
for old crosses erected by Cortez for
his men who died during an early
sojourn on the Baja Peninsula.

Bahía Pichilinque (Peachee-leen-kay) is thought to be the place where Cortez first attempted to establish a colony in 1535. Later it became a haven for pirates who preyed upon the Manila galleons. In recent years, through World War I, the United States maintained a coaling station here for American vessels.

The old pier remains for the pelicans and sea gulls. Boaters find relief in its calm waters from the shifting winds and currents of La Paz harbor nine miles to the south.

The quiet water of Bahía Pichilinque makes this a good place to varnish a boat or to swim in the turquoise waters. It is also a good place to study the pelicans and the flying fish which flip out of the water at sundown.

The surface was so still one night that the reflected stars could be seen in their constellations as clearly in the water as in the sky. Orion's belt and dagger were mirrored there, and the Dipper in the water was turned as if to catch liquid from the Dipper in the sky.

A tiny bright-eyed octopus was found in our bucket of clams gathered at Pichilinque. He was about as big as your thumb and ejected a mass of stringy black "ink" when placed in a pan of water.

Other smaller ones were found clinging to the inside of empty clam shells. They seemed intimidated by the bigger one, darting about and wrapping tiny tenacles around their heads.

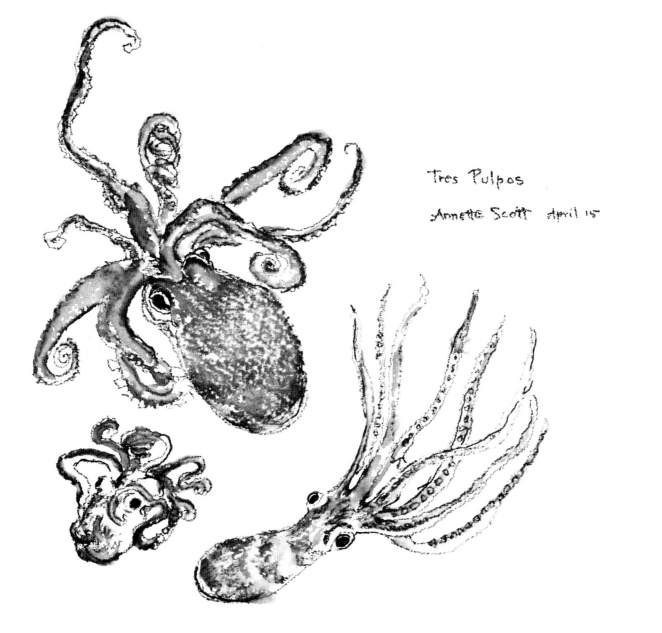

Tres Pulpos

Annette Scott   April 15

Ferry boats run to Guaymas and Mazatlán on the Mexican mainland from Bahía Pichilinque. The trip is an overnight run. On these large ships are staterooms, lounges, a big dining room, and sometimes a dance band of Mexican boys playing American Rock.

La Paz lies nine miles to the south of Bahía Pichilinque. We dropped anchor beside the Alegria *of San Diego.*

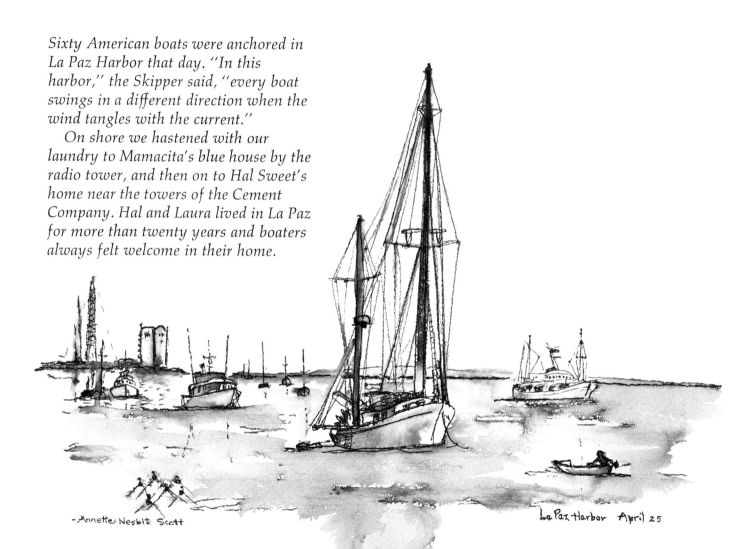

Sixty American boats were anchored in La Paz Harbor that day. "In this harbor," the Skipper said, "every boat swings in a different direction when the wind tangles with the current."

On shore we hastened with our laundry to Mamacita's blue house by the radio tower, and then on to Hal Sweet's home near the towers of the Cement Company. Hal and Laura lived in La Paz for more than twenty years and boaters always felt welcome in their home.

—Annette Nesbit Scott

La Paz Harbor April 25

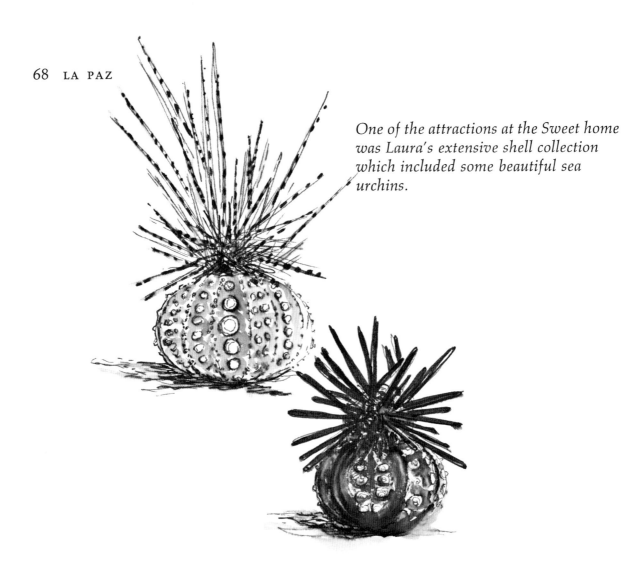

One of the attractions at the Sweet home was Laura's extensive shell collection which included some beautiful sea urchins.

She also collected different kinds of
Brittle Stars.

Is this Sea Horse complaining to the
Puffer Fish?

The pouch of a male Sea Horse is used
to incubate the eggs which the female
deposits there. In due time he gives birth
to the young.

Perhaps he has heard the Skipper's
suggestion that the "pregnant" male Sea
Horse be adopted as the international
symbol for Women's Liberation!

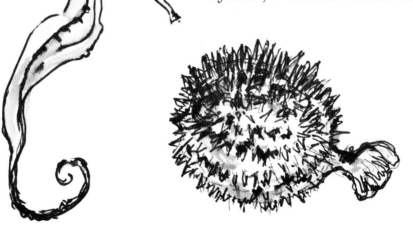

- The Painting Crew

In La Paz on an April day in 1972 we saw a man pick up his mail. His face lit up over an official letter from Mexico City.

He explained that he lived in La Paz and had applied for a registration for his car. He waited patiently for word from Mexico City where registrations were processed. Every six months he was granted a temporary permit to drive in La Paz. Today he had received the long-awaited document — the registration for which he had applied in 1965.

La Perla

Boaters can climb from their shore boats
onto the municipal dock at La Paz. From
there it is a short walk into town to
shop, pick up mail at Oscar Chacón's
office, search for repair supplies, and
perhaps have lunch at La Perla
Restaurant or at Tepepan II along the
waterfront.

Municipal Dock   La Paz

MEMO II
MAZATLAN SIN.

In La Paz Harbor the Marisla II *is bright with new blue paint. She takes passengers into the Gulf for cruises of a week or more, and has been used on several scientific expeditions. Dick and Mary Lou Adcock, who operate her, carry scuba and water skiing gear aboard.*

Movies and underwater photographs have been made from the Marisla II. *A passenger told us he went skin diving and saw fish so numerous they were like a carpet beneath him and like a solid wall around him.*

MARISLA II

Annette Scott

Marisla · La Paz

Freighters like this one were used by the United States during World War II in the south sea islands. Later they were sold to Mexico as surplus.

One of these freighters, carrying drums of high test aviation gasoline, blew up and sank at the municipal dock of La Paz, killing three people and cracking windows for six blocks along the Malacón sea road.

It lay aground obstructing traffic at the pier. Finally, a Mexican tug boat, Protector de Cementos de Pacífico, dragged it out beyond the Topolabampo ferry dock. The top of the hull and the sampson post are still visible in the anchorage.

Remnant

Freighter - Cabo San Lucas 2-11-73

Leaving La Paz we traveled north to Isla
Espíritu Santo and Isla Partida, which
are surrounded by many smaller islands.

The Rooster and the Hen
El Gallo y La Gallina —

El Gallo w. Pelicans
April 30

Ballena Isla
Whale Island - Espiritus Santo

At Partida Cove we saw the Golden Apple *with her red and orange sails furled. She is a Chinese junk, painted black, red, and yellow, with a long green dragon curling along the hull. Tied astern was a small dinghy painted to match.*

The Golden Apple

-Annette Scott

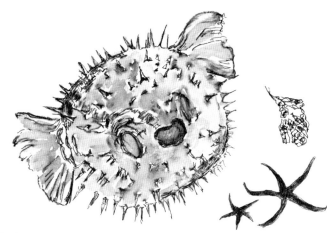

Blowfish
from the Collection of Laura Sweet

The two islands, Espíritu Santo and Partida, are almost connected by a sand bar. The cove between the islands was formed by the eruption and partial sinking of a volcano in the geologic past.

One day in this cove our swim ladder came loose and floated away. Bob Smith of the Rapparee just happened to be rowing by in his dinghy and picked it up. He called to the Skipper, "I'll trade you one swim ladder for a martini!"

- Partida Cove - April 30

There is no indication on the chart of a dangerous reef, covered at high tide, extending from the south end of Isla Partida. Walt and Katie Maertins ''discovered'' this reef when they struck it with their ketch, Evening Star.

Walt was able to get it off the reef without damage, and Katie sent a report to the United States Oceanographic Office. A warning about the reef appeared in the Notice to Mariners *publication and someday ''Katie's Reef'' may be added to the official chart.*

Evening Star at Partida

Some of the navigation charts used in the Gulf were made from Admiral Dewey's surveys on the USS Narrangansett in 1874. The Maertins on Evening Star *made a chart in 1963 of the waters from Isla Partida to Punta San Marcial Rock near Bahía de Agua Verde. They had found no detailed chart available for that area.*

Maertins' chart shows soundings of the depths of all the anchorages in that area and the safe passage round the Gulf side of San Marcial Rock.

Walt and Katie have sailed the Sea of Cortez for over twenty years. Long ago they established the "Chicken Fleet" which travels the safest routes. Walt calls himself "The Big Yellow Rooster, Captain of the Chicken Fleet."

Unknown Waters

Ranch. s. of Nopolo Point

East coast of Baja
3-18-73

Traveling north from Isla Partida we stopped at Isla San Francisco for an hour to enjoy its green water along a sweeping curve of white sand beach. From here the mountains are spectacular along the Baja coastline. High and rugged, they are layered in white, yellow, orange, pink and volcanic black.

As our boat approached Punta Nopolo Sur we saw a small ranch with a clothesline stretched beside a tiny house. Two men rowed out to ask for medicine for their children. They explained by coughing.

We handed a bottle of cough medicine to their boat with a demonstration of how much and how often, so it would not be taken all in one dose! A sack of lollipops was added "to take the taste away."

Entering Caleta San Evaristo the water was rough and the swells big. Dishes slid out of the cupboards, coffee cups jumped from the sink, and the Log Book slid over the instrument panel. We anchored without hitting the sand bar but it was an uneasy anchorage.

Next morning we headed north for

Bahía de Agua Verde, passing Roca Negra and the unexpected two-story house which stands empty just south of the San Carlos anchorage.

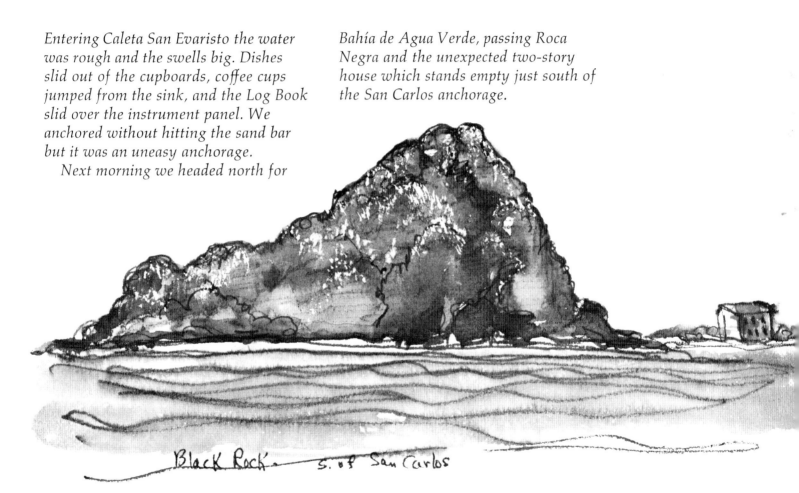

Black Rock.   5.08 San Carlos

Giving San Marcial Rock a very wide berth we circled down into Bahía de Agua Verde, passing the entrance landmark called Solitaria. *Going around the reef, which is nearly covered at high tide, we dropped anchor in the green and turquoise bay.*

Agua Verde   3-15-73

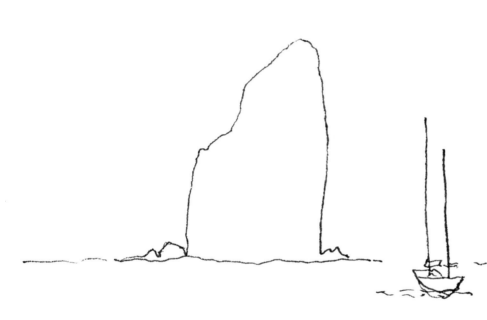

Evening Star by Solitaria
3·17·73

Other boats were anchored in Bahía de Agua Verde: Dreamboat, Miss Salty, Wunderbar, Totem *and* Evening Star. *Bad weather kept us there long enough to visit on each boat.*

Boaters enjoy a special kind of fraternity. Large or small, each boat is the concern of the others. Boaters keep in touch by radio and gather together when chance permits.

Agua Verde 3·15·73

Black Sea Urchins were hiding in the recesses of the tide pools on the reef at Bahía de Agua Verde. A school of fish was trapped in one, an orange starfish in another. These fascinating pools of life are left in the pitted volcanic rocks by the retreating tides.

Tide Pool at Agua Verde

We had the adventure of towing a disabled sail boat into the anchorage at Agua Verde. The water that day was flat and calm — so flat the Skipper said it looked as if it had been ironed. Surfacing whales looked like small black islands, and the silver blades of Manta Rays glittered in the sun.

The sail boat we towed was the Moana, a thirty-four foot ketch manned only by her owner, Ray Quint. The distributor on the motor had failed, and there was no wind. He was trying to sail north to Escondido near the town of Loreto where he could receive repair parts shipped from the States.

Walt and Katie Maertins were anchored at Escondido. While Katie was on the radio trying to locate the repair part and find someone to ship it to Loreto, we took Walt aboard to handle the tow line and went down to find the Moana. We sighted her late in the afternoon just south of the Agua Verde anchorage. Circling close, Walt threw a line to Ray and we towed him into Agua Verde for the night and then north to Escondido the next morning.

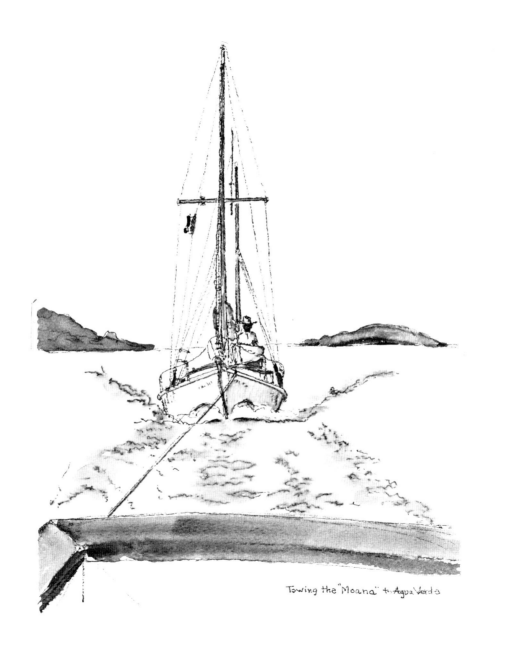

Towing the "Moana" to Agua Verde

Danzante Island 3·17·13
and Candeleros Media

Candeleros Medio · 3·17·73

We threaded our way between small islands called Los Candeleros (The Candlesticks).

There is an uncharted submerged rock, we were told, between the shore and the "Candlestick" nearest to the shore, so we went between the shore candlestick and the middle candlestick. Isla Danzante lies northeast, like a prehistoric lizard.

*Just past Los Candeleros we looked for a
landmark called the "Hound Dog."
Here, the mountains of Escondido, in
shape and muted color looked like
the Grand Canyon transported to the
edge of the sea.*

" Hound Dog" at Escondido - from North

Coyote Bay of Conception

We continued north and passed the historic old town of Loreto. Soon we saw the striking rock formations of Bahía San Juanico. To the north of this is a huge landfall which marks the Punta Púlpito anchorage. There we saw a full orange moon float up from the water as we lay anchored in the black shadow of the headland.

Sea Gipsy sailed in the next morning with a water-maker problem. The Skipper explained by radio what he thought would get it started. His directions were followed, and Sea Gipsy reported happily that the machine was again making distilled water.

Above Púlpito we dipped south into Bahía Concepción. We passed the place where the Skipper had once discovered a pinnacle lying dangerously near the surface. Traveling there years ago on a fishing trip, he saw the reading on the depth indicator jump suddenly from ninety feet to six feet and back to ninety feet again. He stopped, turned, verified its location in mid-channel, and reported it to the U.S. Hydrographic Office. The spot is now marked on the navigation chart.

Staying clear of the long shafts of

green water which mark the shoals, we anchored in Coyote Cove. It was Eastertime, and we shared a ham dinner and hand-painted Easter eggs with friends on the Maree Sea.

Rock in San Juanico Cove

*A velvet sombrero-shaped hill is a
landmark for the old town of Mulegé
north of Bahía Concepción. An
afternoon's run took us beyond the town
to Punta Chivata. Winds and rough
water made anchoring difficult that day,
but we were determined to make the
beach in our dory and go in to dinner at
the Hotel Borrego de Oro.*

*Carrying our shoes we jumped from
the dory onto the wet beach. After a
good dinner we returned in velvet
darkness to our cruiser, under a sky full
of stars.*

Hotel Borrego de Oro - Inez Point

Santa Rosalía has an enclosed harbor formed by a breakwater built of molded blocks of slag from the town's copper smelter. At times the wind can blow across the town from the west with enough force to loosen anchors from the soft bottom mud. We woke one morning to find our boat broadside against the breakwater!

Santa Rosalia - Good Friday April 20, 1973

Santa Rosalia

Mexican men from a barge and tug boat offered their help, and by nine o'clock we were pulled off and re-anchored. Rob Reed and Pat Mead, two teens from a nearby sailboat, put on their scuba gear and inspected the bottom of our boat. They scraped off lots of barnacles but saw no damage to the hull.

In the 1880's Santa Rosalía's copper mines produced three thousand tons a month. All the fuel was brought from Europe around the Horn in square rigged sailing ships.

The copper mine was then a French operation. A church and all the buildings in the town were prefabricated in Europe. The sections were brought around the Horn and bolted together. The church still serves the town, and work continues at the smelter although it is now under Mexican operation. French bread is still baked from the original recipes in the same brick ovens built by the French founders of the city.

Old Church at Santa Rosalia

Crossing the Sea of Cortez from Santa Rosalía we were guided by the unmistakable peaks of Las Tetas de Cabra. Coming closer, the whole formation looked somewhat like a sleeping dragon.

Turning left from the harbor entrance at Guaymas, we anchored in the Las Playitas anchorage beside the Sea Gipsy.

The Sleeping Dragon

"Sea Gipsy" at Guaymas

The restaurant of Las Playitas Motel is brilliant with sunshine through yellow windows. Thousands of sea shells and bright crepe paper flowers decorate the walls and hang from the ceiling. Olga is a waitress there who liked this sketch and put her autograph on it.

Olga

Las Playitas Dining Room - Guaymas
- Annette Scott April 9 - 1972

*The wrought-iron tracery of a bandstand
in a small plaza facing a church can be
found in almost any city in Mexico. This
one is in Guaymas. The boys who were
replacing the light bulbs walked over to
see this sketch and spelled out the
various names which identify the spot.*

Manuel ui Juan

Kiosko Plaza Tres de Julio

Castillo de Guaymas

San Fernando Church

by Annette Scott
April 8 - 1972

The Charl Don, *formerly owned by the Skipper, was at anchor off the Colonia Península in Guaymas.*

Men have a feeling for boats they have owned and operated. The Skipper put it this way:

You work on a boat till you know every bolt and rib. Your family and your friends have good times and adventures on her. When you sell her you want the new owner to take care of her and maintain her. Looking back as you leave her, there is the feeling somehow that you are leaving a part of yourself.

Leaving Guaymas we retraced our route through the turquoise waters of the Gulf to the southern tip of Baja. At Cabo San Lucas we topped the water tanks and fueled for the return trip to San Diego. ¡Adiós y hasta la vista! Goodby till we see you again!

Hope it's soon!